WINNIE-T...
LITTL...
feng shui

Inspired by A. A. Milne & Illustrated by E. H. Shepard

First published in Great Britain 1999
Printed under the Methuen imprint
by Egmont Children's Books Limited
239 Kensington High Street, London W8 6SA
Copyright © 1999 Michael John Brown, Peter Janson-Smith,
Roger Hugh Vaughan Charles Morgan and Timothy Michael Robinson,
Trustees of the Pooh Properties.
Adapted from *Winnie-the-Pooh, The House at Pooh Corner,*
Now We Are Six and *When We Were Very Young*
text by A.A. Milne and line illustrations by E.H. Shepard
copyright under the Berne Convention
Devised and written by Anna Ludlow
Book design by Karina Edginton-Vigus
copyright © 1999 Egmont Children's Books Limited

3 5 7 9 10 8 6 4

ISBN 0 416 19650 0

Printed in Hong Kong

HOW IT ALL BEGAN

When I told Pooh that I was writing a book about Feng Shui, Pooh said, "Oh," and "Are you?" and after a long, thoughtful pause he said, "Fung what?"

"Feng Shui," I said. "It's the ancient Chinese system of living life in harmony with your environment and with the natural rhythms of nature, and of making use of the dynamic flow of energy in the universe, to bring you greater happiness and good fortune."

"Oh," said Pooh, and he thought how wonderful it would be to have a Real Brain that told you things about ancient rhythms and Chinese fortunes. And then he asked carelessly, "Will I be in it anywhere?"

And when I said, "Yes, because living in harmony with nature is what Bears do Best," Pooh said to himself, "A book about me. How grand!"

Then Piglet, who had been listening all along, asked whether he would be in the book, too.

"Yes, of course," I said, "because bringing happiness to others is what Piglets do Best."

But now, before all the others start asking whether they are in it too, I think perhaps we'd better begin.

WHAT BEARS DO BEST

The ancient Chinese system of feng shui
can appear complicated at first.

Even a bit abstract.

Chinese symbols are not always easy to interpret.

Especially for a bear of very little brain.

Feng shui is about what bears do best,
creating balance by being in harmony with nature.

The principles are really very simple to apply,
almost as instinctive as humming a new hum.

Not that Pooh really knows this, because Pooh is a Bear of Very Little Brain and long words Bother him. In fact, *nobody* in the forest really seems to *know* what feng shui is. Everybody just knew one day that it was *there*. They didn't know where it had come from, or when it had arrived, it was just there.

WHEN FENG SHUI CAME TO
THE HUNDRED ACRE WOOD

It was Rabbit who came across it first. One day, he
saw the words 'feng shui' written on a Notice and he
decided that it must have something to do
with what Christopher Robin did on Tuesdays.
Rabbit thought that if only he could *find*
Christopher Robin, perhaps he could tell Rabbit
who or what feng shui was.

But since it *was* Tuesday, and Christopher Robin
had already gone out, Rabbit went
to ask Owl instead.

Owl, being Clever, told Rabbit that feng shui is
pronounced 'foong shway'. And he looked
Very Wise Indeed when he told Rabbit that it meant
'wind and water', but he couldn't explain *exactly*
what it was all about, because Rabbit was looking
over his shoulder in an impatient kind of way
and making him nervous.
But he told Rabbit that he thought feng shui
could be found in the Forest.
"Ah," said Rabbit, and off he went,
to ask Pooh if he'd seen it.

"Pooh," asked Rabbit. "Have you seen a feng shui in the Forest at all?"
"No," said Pooh, "not a - no," said Pooh. "I saw Tigger just now."
"That's no good," said Rabbit.

"A feng shui?" thought Pooh to himself.
And then he began to wonder if
a hum about it might come to him,
with words that rhymed with 'shway'.

"Piglet, have you seen a feng shui
in the Forest?" Rabbit asked Piglet.
"N - no," said Piglet.
"Isn't that one of the Fiercer Animals?"
"That's what I'm trying to find out, Piglet,"
said Rabbit, importantly.

"They haven't got any Brains, any of them,"
thought Eeyore, sighing to himself.
"Isn't anyone going to ask me?" he said,
to anyone who was listening.
"Always the last to be asked," said Eeyore bitterly.

But perhaps, dear reader, while Rabbit is busy
looking for feng shui, I should tell you
some of the things about it that have been
found in the Forest, such as how chi flows
and how to balance yin and yang,
how to choose a good place to build your home
and how to be in harmony with nature ...

THE FLOW OF CHI

Chi is the flow of energy.
Chi can flow up ...

... Or down

Chi can be auspicious.

Or inauspicious.

Sleeping with your head towards the east
encourages the best flow of chi
to ensure a restful night.

Mirrors facing the bed upset the flow of chi during the night, disturbing a good night's rest, and can make you, and any guests who might be staying, feel restless.

Feng shui is about harnessing the forces
of energy in nature to be of beneficial effect
to you and your environment.

Sheng Chi is good chi. It is created
by energy that flows in a meandering fashion.
Gently meandering water creates good chi,
and is especially helpful for playing Poohsticks.

Fast-flowing water is not auspicious.

Too much of it can result in the need for rescue.

Shar Chi is bad chi.
Sharp, spiky things, like gorse bushes,
create Shar Chi, and are best avoided.

"Do you think honey can make sheng chi?"
said Pooh to Eeyore.
"Honey flows gently ..." said Pooh, thoughtfully.
"... And I think I have something Very Important
to do," he said, going home to do it.

"And I suppose sharp, spiky thistles make shar chi," said Eeyore gloomily, waving a hoof at a patch he had saved. "Huh!" he said, and he humped off.

It isn't so funny that a bear likes honey,
Buzz! Buzz! Buzz! Now we know why he does!

BALANCING YIN AND YANG

Yin and yang are opposites.
Yang is active.

Yin is passive.

A good balance of yin and yang is essential.
Too much yang energy can cause accidents ...

... And confusion ...

... Even nightmares.

Too much noise creates an excess of yang and can upset the neighbours.

Worraworraworraworraworra.

"What did you say it was?" asked Eeyore.

"Tigger."

"Ah!" said Eeyore.

"He's just come," explained Piglet.

"Ah!" said Eeyore again.

He thought for a long time and then said:

"When is he going?"

Yang is hot.
Yin is cold.
Too much yin energy can lead to ...

Physical inactivity ...

... an accumulation of coldness ...

... and a gloomy state of mind.

Water is one of the best cures
for too much yang energy.
Its calming influence can help create
a better balance of yin and yang.

But those who are by nature very yin
develop a life-long antipathy towards water.

They simply can't be expected to
appreciate the benefits.

Those who are *excessively* yin
should try and keep away from water altogether.

Wearing red is a very helpful cure for
too much yin energy.

It's surprising how a red ribbon
can turn your bad mood on its head.

"LET'S BUILD IT HERE," SAID POOH.

If your home is in a place
where the air is stale, where the land is damp
and boggy, and where the winds are harsh and
threatening, it will not be a happy home.
Feng shui would advise having your house moved
to another part of the forest altogether.

A well-positioned home will be auspicious
and bring happiness to its owner.
Trees behind a house give it support
for good fortune and happiness, while gently
undulating land, and open space
in front of a house, bring good luck.

"We will build it here," said Pooh,
"just by this wood, out of the wind,
because this is where I thought of it."

Some friends can never
be relied on to
accept gifts graciously.
But if your gift is
based on the
principles of
feng shui, you may
get a surprisingly
positive response.

"Here it is as
good as ever,"
said Eeyore.
"In fact,
better in places."
"Much better,"
said Pooh
and Piglet
together.

If your home is in a green and luscious part of the forest, chi can wrap itself around your house, bringing you good luck.

Places that face the direction of a warm breeze
have excellent feng shui.

But a blustery place is *not* blessed with good feng shui.

If you like visitors, arranging your furniture in a friendly way will create a good flow of chi, making visitors feel welcome and completely at ease.

If you don't like visitors, uncomfortable surroundings will upset the chi, ensuring that your visitors don't stay for long.

If your visitors don't get the message, fill your house
with clutter before they next visit.
A cluttered house creates an excess of yang energy
and makes the chi flow the wrong way.

Don't take your evasive techniques too far –
if the yang energy is *very* excessive,
your home may not last.

MAKING A GRAND ENTRANCE

A welcoming light outside your
front door will ward off negative chi,
and encourage friends to visit ...

... day and night.

A front door by a sharp incline ...

... is very inauspicious.

The size of a door is very important.
Large spacious doors invite good fortune.

And friendly visitors.

Small doors bring bad luck,
and visitors who won't leave,
even when you've asked them politely.

A doorbell creates a good flow of chi.

Unless it belongs to someone else ...

... and they are feeling lost without it.

BEING IN HARMONY WITH NATURE

The elements of nature need to be
in balance to create good feng shui.
If the elements of nature are not in balance, it may
attract the wrong sort of bees into the forest.
And as Pooh has discovered, the wrong sort of bees
make the wrong sort of honey.
And when *that* happens, the feng shui
is not good *at all*.

Nature is cyclical.
So are woozle footprints.

Overhead beams and protrusions are inauspicious.
Being underneath them may cause anxiety,
and can even be dangerous to your health.

If you come from a hot climate, you will probably have an excitable, changeable nature.

If you come from a grey, damp climate,
you will probably have a grey, damp nature —
don't try and fight it.

If you come from a hot climate,
you may not find those from a grey,
damp climate always welcome your enthusiasm.

Avoid ...

... being exposed ...

... to the elements.

Especially if you already know you don't like them.

If you want to be happy ...

... follow your instincts.

FRIENDLIER WITH TWO

If you are looking for friendship, display personal items of sentimental value in pairs in your home.

A single pot of honey is a lonely pot of honey.
It's always friendlier with two.

IT WAS HERE ALL ALONG

"Rabbit," said Pooh. "It's been found."

"What has?" said Rabbit.

"Fung ... that thing you were
looking for," said Pooh.

"Where is it now?" asked Rabbit.

"Well, I think it's been seen all over
the Forest," said Pooh.

"Then it could be anywhere, now," said Rabbit.

"We better go and tell Christopher Robin.
Are you coming, Pooh?"

"I don't think so," said Pooh. "It's nearly eleven o'clock, and I have to go home and do one or two things. Because I haven't done them yet."

So Pooh went home to do them.

If you want to bring the benefits of feng shui into *your* life, and live in harmony with nature, do as Pooh does, and find a warm and sunny spot to sit in a quiet part of the Forest.

If you spend enough time in that calm and peaceful place, you will find much happiness comes your way.

THIS WARM AND SUNNY SPOT

This warm and sunny Spot
Belongs to Pooh.
And here he wonders what
He's going to do.
Oh, bother I forgot —
It's Piglet's too.

A. A. MILNE

A. A. Milne, born in 1882, wrote his stories about
Winnie-the-Pooh for his son Christopher Robin.
The characters in the stories were based on
Christopher Robin's real nursery toys, and their
adventures are set in Ashdown Forest,
where the family lived.

E. H. SHEPARD

E. H. Shepard, born in 1879, became known as 'The man
who drew Pooh'. His witty and affectionate illustrations
of Pooh and his friends from the Hundred Acre Wood
are an inseparable part of the appeal of the stories.